WRITER'S BREAKTHROUGH

Steps to Copyright and Publish Your Own Book

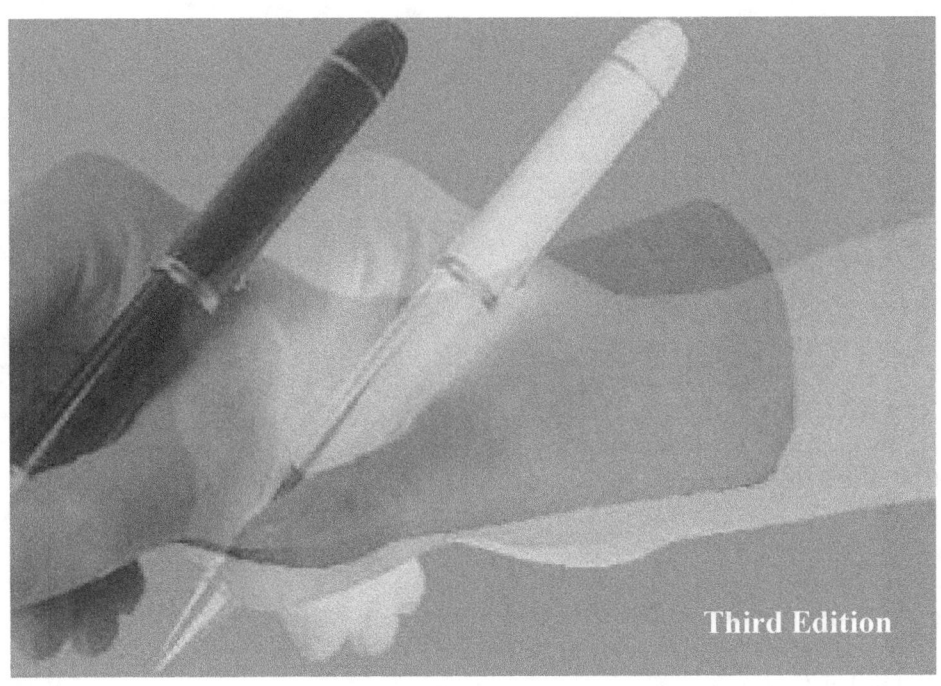

Third Edition

Grace LaJoy Henderson

***Inspirations** by Grace LaJoy*

Raymore, MO 64083
E-mail: poetry@gracelajoy.com
Website: www.gracelajoy.com

Cover by Grace LaJoy Henderson

WRITER'S BREAKTHROUGH
Copyright © 2013 by Grace LaJoy Henderson
Published by Inspirations by Grace
Raymore, MO 64083

Library of Congress Control Number: 2012918004

ISBN 978-0-9829404-4-0

All rights reserved. No portion of this book may be copied, reproduced or transmitted in any form without prior written permission from the publisher.

Printed in the United States of America

PREFACE

The purpose of this book is to educate you as a writer about the basic information needed to copyright and publish your own writings. The information in this book will certainly get you off to a running start to understanding the steps required to copyright and publish your book!

I am rapidly becoming an expert in the self-publishing field. I *have* authored and published several books and there are more to come! Furthermore, while I do not claim to know everything about copyrighting and publishing, I have compiled the information that I **do** have in order to lead writers who know nothing into the right direction.

My desire is to teach you the basics about registering your copyright, as well as share EVERYTHING that I have learned up to this point about book publishing. I strongly believe that anyone who has a gift to write should also be armed with the information needed to copyright and publish their writings. Furthermore, a gifted writer should not have to pay thousands of dollars for self-publishing unless they CHOOSE to.

This book will save you time and money! How? Well, the more you learn from this book, the less time you will spend researching and asking questions; and the more of the publishing process that you are able to do for yourself, the less money you will have to pay someone else to do for you.

DEDICATION

To all of you gifted writers who have longed to find a way to share your gift with the world. Your time has come!

ACKNOWLEDGMENTS

I acknowledge Dr. Zalmer J. Nichols, Chancellor of Faith Bible College, who encouraged me to "build a course" and inspired me to teach students of the college how to publish their own books.

TESTIMONIALS

"Writer's Breakthrough is an excellent, practical, easy-to-understand resource for novice writers and aspiring self-publishers." --Midwest Book Review

"This book has been a great help to my students who showed interest in becoming an author." Dr. Gwendolyn Squires, Public School Principal - Kansas City, Missouri

"It is an answer to prayer. I was seeking direction for the next steps and <u>all</u> of my answers were found in this material." G. Lakes, Jr.

"The content was easy to understand and grasp. This book made me feel empowered to achieve my purpose...." C. Price

"It is an invaluable tool worth more than the asking price." R. Bradley

Table of Contents

Section #	Section Title	Section Page #
	Introduction	7
	Foreword	8
1	A personal word to the aspiring author	9
2	Registering Your Copyright	11
3	What Does The Word "Publish" Mean?	15
4	Traditional Publishing -vs- Self Publishing	17
5	Producing Your Book	19
6	Your ISBN	27
7	Your Bar Code	28
8	Your Pre-assigned Control Number	28
9	Printing Your Book	29
10	Distributing Your Book	30
11	Marketing Your Book	32
12	Self-publishing Your E-book	33
13	Resources for Writers	37
14	Other Helpful Resources	38
15	Helpful Websites	39

Exhibits A-P — **41-65**
Glossary — **67**
Index — **68-69**
Other Books and Resources *by Dr. Grace LaJoy Henderson* — **70**

INTRODUCTION

I can remember the days when I had a lot of inspired writings, but, did not have any idea what to do with them. People would tell me that my writing ability could make me money, but no one could tell me HOW. People who did not know the answers would tell me to "go to the internet...." but, when I asked, "where on the internet should I go?" they did not have a clue. These well-meaning people were sincerely trying to encourage me, but they just did not know how to lead, guide, or direct me.

Well, this book will teach you *exactly* what websites to go to, addresses to write to, and phone numbers to call. After reading this book, you will know exactly how to copyright your poems, books, and other writings. You will also know the steps necessary to publish your own book.

After reading this book you may still choose to utilize a professional self-publisher to publish your book, but, with this information you will be empowered to make an *educated* decision about how much of the work you may want to do for yourself and how much of the work you may *choose* to hire a professional self-publisher to do for you. This information will also help you to understand exactly what the book publisher is doing for you and exactly what you are being billed for.

Other self-publishing books may have anywhere from 300 to over 500 pages of information, which can be overwhelming for the beginning author who knows nothing about self-publishing. Writer's Breakthrough offers you a book that is short, simple, easy to read and to understand, as well as informative; a book that will motivate and encourage you to get started using your writing talent immediately!

FOREWORD

While many aspects of publishing are the same for every book, many of the views expressed in this book about how a book should be formatted are the opinion of Grace LaJoy Henderson. They are based on her own personal book publishing experience, which included research on the way other writers and publishers have chosen to format their own books. These rules are based on the publishing of books with several chapters (books similar to Grace LaJoy Henderson's own book, <u>A Gifted Child in Foster Care: A Story of Resilience</u>). Other types of books may require different types of formatting.

The purpose of these book-writing guidelines is to give the writer who knows <u>nothing</u> a place to begin. Once the writing/publishing process has begun, the writer may add some ideas and creativity of his/her own. The writer is encouraged to be as creative and as innovative as he/she wishes to be during the book publishing process. The goal of this book is to motivate writers and encourage them to get started and to make real progress on their goal of publishing their first book.

Writers may choose to follow the guidelines in this book or they may choose to do some more research of their own to find out exactly what other publishers have done and what has worked for other writers. If a writer does decide to do research on other authors, they are encouraged to only do research on books that are top quality, best sellers.

1 A PERSONAL WORD TO THE ASPIRING AUTHOR

People have asked me to look at their writing and tell them if I think that it is good. I do not believe in telling someone whether their writing is good or bad. If you have been inspired to write something and you *know* beyond a shadow of a doubt that it will benefit others, then who am I to tell you if it is good or bad? I am not an editor <u>and</u> I have no right to, nor do I desire to, "judge" what someone else has been inspired to write.

The questions I would ask are: Are you absolutely, positively sure that this writing is part of your purpose? Will it help, encourage, or empower someone else? If the answer to these two questions is "yes" then you do not need validation from any person. The only thing you need is to begin the publishing process. However, when you begin going through the publishing process you will need, among other things, a good editor.

An editor may be able to tell you how to make your work more acceptable to the world or readers by correcting errors in grammar, misspelled words, or changing the way something is said (without changing the message) so that your words will not offend or turn your readers off. Your goal should be to edify and uplift your readers and not to upset or offend them. This is where a good editor may be helpful.

You have the power to do anything! If you have a gift to write, then use it! If you have been inspired to write something that will affect others in a positive way, share it! Do not wait around for someone to discover you or your work. Do everything within your power to make your work available to as many people as possible…but not before you register your *copyright*.

2   REGISTERING YOUR COPYRIGHT

I suggest that you register your writings with the Library of Congress before sharing them with anyone, especially before allowing anyone to have a copy of your work. In this section, you will be introduced to the basics of registering your copyright based on information from the United States Copyright Office. This section will teach you:

- *Why you should register with the United States Office of Copyrights*
- *Exactly how to register*
- *About registering electronically (online)*
- *The advantages of registering electronically (online)*
- *The cost of registering*
- *How long the copyright process takes*
- *About the "poor man's copyright"*

Why should I register my copyright with the United States Copyright Office?

Many people believe that you must "copyright" your work in order for it to belong to you. But, contrary to popular belief, your work belongs to you from the *very moment that you create it*. Circular 1 – <u>Copyright Basics</u>, published by the United States Copyright Office, says this: "the moment that you put your work in a tangible format" you own the copyright to it. But, it also states that, while registering your copyright is not a requirement for protection, there are some advantages to registering your copyright. The advantages include, but are not limited to, the following:

- Registering your copyright allows your ownership of your creation to become public record. You are telling the world that "this work belongs to me".

-If someone infringes on your copyright and you desire to sue them in court for it, your work will need to be registered with the copyright office. Your copyright certificate serves as evidence of your copyright claim.

There is an exception to the creator/ownership rule. That exception is a <u>"Work Made For Hire"</u>. Circular 9 states that when a work is Made For Hire then "the employer, not the employee, is considered the author." "The employer may be a firm, an organization, or an individual."

For <u>everything</u> you need to know about the copyright law, including all forms and publications go online to <u>www.copyright.gov</u>.

How do I register my copyright with the United States Copyright Office?

To register your copyright with the United States Copyright Office, you should submit *three* things to the copyright office:

- A completed copyright application **[see Exhibits A & B]**
- A non-refundable fee (payable to 'Register of Copyrights')
- A non-returnable copy of your work that you are requesting registration for

Place these three items in an envelope and mail them to:

U.S. Copyright Office
101 Independent Ave. S.E.
Washington, D.C. 20559-6000

How much does it cost to register my copyright?

At the time of publication of the version of "Writer's Breakthrough", the fee for copyright registration by mail was $65. Which is considerably higher than the fee of $35 to register electronically (online).

How do I register my work electronically (online)

The U. S. Copyright office now offers writers the option to register their copyright electronically with the Electronic Copyright Office (eCO) at www.copyright.gov. They recommend using this online system in lieu of mailing in a paper copyright form.

But, before using the online copyright system, please be aware of the acceptable file types that can be submitted (in lieu of a hard copy book). I highly recommend .pdf (Portable Document Format), but, other acceptable file types are:

.doc (Microsoft Word Document)
.docx (Microsoft Word Open XML Document)
.htm, .html (HyperText Markup Language)
.rtf (Rich Text Document)
.txt (Text File)
.wpd (WordPerfect Document)
.wps (Microsoft Works Word Processor Document)

The U. S. Copyright office encourages writers to review this list carefully before uploading an electronic file. They will not accept files that are not in one of the acceptable formats.

How will I benefit by registering my work electronically (online)

Some advantages to registering your copyright online, as opposed to mailing a hardcopy are:

- There is a lower filing fee to register on line.
- The processing time is faster.
- The status of your submission can be tracked online.
- The filing fee can be paid securely, with a credit or debit card or an electronic check.

How long does it take to receive my copyright certificate?

The time required to process your copyright request may vary depending on the number of copyright applicants at the time you submit yours. At the time of the publication of this version of "Writer's Breakthrough", the average processing time for electronic filing is 2.5 months; and the average time for processing mailed paper forms is 6.5 months.

What is the Poor Man's Copyright?

Many people who cannot afford to pay the fee to register their copyright with the United States Copyright Office have been known to utilize the "poor man's copyright". This simply means that a person places their work in an envelope, addresses the envelope to themselves, places their own address in the sender's address spot, puts a stamp on the envelope, and mails the envelope (with their work in it) back to themselves. When the envelope comes back in the mail, it should not be opened, but, placed in a safe place. The envelope would only be opened by a judge in court if the owner of the work ever needed to prove to a court of law that the work in the envelope belongs to them.

Many people believe that the "poor man's copyright" is enough to prove that they created the work and that they are the owners. However, according to the Frequently Asked Questions section on the United States Copyright Office website, "there is no provision in the copyright law regarding any such type of protection, and it is <u>not</u> a substitute for registration".

I personally do a "poor man's copyright" on virtually every writing that I create *and* I also register my work with the United States Copyright Office.

3   WHAT DOES THE WORD *PUBLISH* MEAN?

According to the United States Copyright Office, to *publish* means "to distribute copies or phonorecords of a work to the public by sale or other transfer of ownership, or by rental, lease or lending" "A work is also *published* if there has been an offer to distribute copies or phonorecords to a group of persons for the purposes of further distribution, public performance, or public display". My personal definition of the word *publish* is "to make your work available to the world".

Many writers who know nothing about book publishing believe that the professional printing of a book means that the book has been *published*. For example, after I completed the publishing of my first book, many people asked me, "Who published your book?" When I told them that I published it they asked again, "no, I mean who *published* it? Then I would tell them again, "I published my book myself". Then they would say, "I mean who *printed* it?" Now, *that* is an entirely different question! The truth is that printing usually occurs *during* the process of publishing, but printing, in itself, is not publishing. There are several steps to book publishing and I will discuss them later in this book. But, for now I will tell you about the different types of publishing that are available to you as a writer.

4   TRADITIONAL PUBLISHING -VS- SELF PUBLISHING

Submitting your book to a Traditional Publisher

When you submit your book to a book publisher, they may review your book. If they choose to publish your book, they may ask you to sign your copyright over to them. They will then do all of the work and pay all of the costs related to publishing your book. They will also do all of the advertising and marketing of your book. Then, they will pay you a royalty for each book sold.

One pitfall to submitting your work to book publishers is that they only choose a limited number of new author's books per year and are very selective in what books they choose to publish. So, unless you are a celebrity author, a traditional publisher may not have an interest in choosing your book for publication. One positive thing about submitting your book to traditional book publishers is that if by chance they *do* choose to publish your book, they pay for everything and they usually have all of the resources needed to make your book available to the world.

Self Publishing

There are two ways to self publish: 1) Hire a professional. 2) Do it yourself. If you choose to hire a professional you will need lots of money to pay for their knowledge and expertise.

Professional Self-Publishers do everything that traditional book publishers do for you. The differences are that you *pay them* to publish your book for you and *you* retain all copyrights to your book. Another difference is that you must do your own advertising and marketing. (Some professional self-publishers may advertise and market your book for you for a fee)

So that you may begin selling your book, most self-publishers will supply you with a certain number of your books to begin with (included in your price), and thereafter you pay the professional self-publisher an agreed-upon amount per book if you need more books in the future. One good thing about choosing a professional self-publisher is that they usually have the expertise as well as the resources already in place to handle all of your book *publishing needs. One thing to consider, however, when utilizing a professional self-publisher is that they likely will not give you a copy of your book on a computer disk, and so they will be the only ones who will be able to make additional prints of your book. It may cost less per book if you get your books printed for yourself, because when a professional self-publisher supplies you with copies of your book, they will increase the price slightly so that they may always make a profit off of the sale of your book.*

The only way to end up with a copy of your book on a disk for yourself is to **publish your book yourself** without the help of any type of a professional book publisher.

The steps involved in publishing your book yourself are:

Producing your book

Getting your ISBN

Getting your Bar Code

Getting your Library of Congress Pre-assigned Control Number

Printing your book

Copyrighting your book (discussed earlier)

Distributing your book

Marketing your book

The good thing about both types of self-publishing is that you do not have to wait around for a traditional book publisher to "discover" your talent. If you know that you have created a successful piece of material, then you may initiate the publishing of your work on your own through self-publishing.

Regardless of how you go about getting your book published, you will be expected to make appearances, such as radio, television, conferences, and other events in order to let others know that your book is available for purchase.

5 PRODUCING YOUR BOOK

When I was going through the process of publishing my first book, I looked on my bookshelf and pulled off all of the most popular best sellers that I had purchased. I then patterned my book after them. Everything that these books included, I found out what it meant and made sure that my book displayed the *exact same* details and professionalism. For example, in examining books that had sold over a million copies, I found that most Christian authors stated the type of bible that their scripture texts came out of. Even though I did not understand why they did that, I put the type of Bible that *my* scripture texts came from in my book. Also, I notice that this statement was usually placed on the page behind the inside cover page, and so, *this* is where I placed mine. After all, I was creating a book that I desired to sale to millions and so if I wanted to create a "million dollar book" then I had to pattern it after the books of authors who had already sold over a million copies! However, the *content* of my book is all my own creativity; the poems, the writings, the inspirational messages, etc.

Producing your book includes:

Designing your book cover (front cover, back cover, spine)

Preparing material for the inside pages of your book

Designing your book cover

Producing your book includes designing a book cover. Your book cover is your reader's first impression of your book. Sometimes people will become interested in the inside content of your book just because of the way that it is introduced and presented on the cover. However, you must be sure that what you say about your book on the cover genuinely reflects what the reader will find inside of the book.

Book covers consist of three parts:

A front cover

A back cover

A spine.

The front cover

The front cover usually includes a title, a subtitle, the author's name, and some type of cover art. The words of the title should be large enough to be seen from far away. The subtitle is usually words that give readers a better understanding of what your title means or why you chose the title that you chose. For example, my book title is More Than Mere Words, and my subtitle is *Poetry That Ministers!* I entitled my book More Than Mere Words because the writings in it are more than mere words; the writings are words of poetry and inspiration that were designed to actually *minister* to those that read them.

The author's name is usually at the bottom center of the front cover, however, it may be creatively placed anywhere the author chooses to place it. Finally, your cover art should be something that represents the title as well as the content of the book. This is only the minimum that the reader should find on the front cover of a book. An author may be creative and add anything he/she chooses to their book cover. My suggestion would be to keep the front cover simple, without too much writing. The front cover should have only enough writing and information to encourage the reader to want to know more about the book. **[see Exhibit C]**

The back cover

The title of the book should be placed on the back cover and the font (lettering) type should be the same as the front cover. The size and color of the title can be different than the front cover. The back cover should also include a brief synopsis of the book. A synopsis lets the reader know what the book is about and what the reader can expect to gain by reading the book. The back cover is a good spot to identify your target audience, for example, *"If you are a married person who is contemplating leaving your spouse, this book will give you options of some things that you may do in order to try to stay together before making that final heart-wrenching decision."*

The back cover may also include a picture of the author, and/or a very, very short biography about the author. The short biography may include other books written by the author and/or a little bit about the author's education and training…something very short that tell the reader what qualifies the author to write on the subject of the book. It is also appropriate to put testimonials about the book on the back cover.

The bottom of the back cover should include the name and logo of the publishing company, the barcode, and the ISBN. **[see Exhibit D]**

The spine

The spine should include the book's title, the author's name, and the publishing company's logo. It is suggested that the title have the same font type as the back and front covers. The publishing company's name and/or logo should be at the bottom end of the spine. **[see Exhibit E]**

Preparing material for the inside pages of your book

Producing a book includes preparing material that will be on the inside pages of the book.

The inside pages include the following:

The title page

The copyright page

The page after the copyright page

The introduction page

The pages in-between

The final pages

The title page

The very first page of the book should be the *title page*. The title page should include the words of the title and the sub-title. It should also include the name, city and state of the publisher along with the publisher's logo or symbol. The title page may include the exact same picture or design that is on the cover or it can just include only the words from the cover. The same font style as the front cover may also be used on the title page, but this is not necessary. **[see Exhibit F]**

The copyright page

The other side of the title page is called the credits or *Copyright Page*. This page includes any disclaimers, credits, and copyrights. It also includes the Library of Congress Pre-assigned Control Number (PCN) and the ISBN *(discussed in sections 6 & 8)*. In addition, this is the page where the reader can be reminded that this work may not be copied without the written permission of the publisher as well as how to contact the publisher to request permission. A statement of what country your book was printed in should be present on this page as well. **[see Exhibit G]**

The copyright page also includes the book title, author's name, publisher's name and address, and the year of the copyright of the book.

The page after the copyright page

The page after the copyright page may be used in a number of ways. I personally used this page in my first book to tell my readers why I wrote the book. However this page has been used for things such as *acknowledgements, dedications, testimonials*, a *preface*, or a *foreword*. This page may also be used for a *table of contents*.

Acknowledgements may consist of the author thanking those who have played an integral part in their life or those who have inspired or encouraged the author to follow the author's dream to write the book. The author may acknowledge family members, teachers, their pastor, their church, other authors who they have looked up to and or have been inspired by, those who assisted them in the publishing process of their book, or anyone else whom the author deems as worthy of acknowledgment. **[see Exhibit H1]**

Dedications. The author may choose to dedicate their book to someone very special in their life. This is usually someone whom the author loves very much, such as a spouse or a child (or children); Someone whom the author shares a personal or intimate relationship with; Someone who has offered emotional support as well as exhibited patience during the publishing of the book; Someone who has been directly affected by the long hours that the author spent on the production of the book. The author may dedicate the book to *anyone* whom he/she chooses. **[see Exhibit H2]**

Testimonials are written by others who have read your book and have something positive to say about it. In order to place testimonials in a book, one or more people should be allowed to read it <u>before</u> the printing is complete. **[see Exhibit H3]**

The *Preface* or *Foreword* is one or more paragraphs written about either the author and/or the contents of the book. It may be written by the author or by someone other than the author. **[see Exhibit H4 and H5]**

Note: A well-known individual or an expert on the subject of the book would be a good place to start when considering acknowledgements, testimonials, prefaces, and forewords. However, the best contributor will be the individual who has read your book and was so sincerely impressed or inspired by it that he/she <u>offered</u> a to write something about the book without being asked.

The *Table of Contents* is an outline, which tells the reader what is in the book, what order the contents may be found, and the page numbers the contents may be found on. **[see Exhibit H6]**

The introduction page

At this point a decision has probably been made about what will be placed on the first few pages and the order in which the items will be placed. The next page is the *Introduction Page*. The introduction page is written by the author and introduces the book and its contents to the readers. The introduction should tell the reader several things: The purpose of the book, why the author wrote the book, what the book is all about, what the reader can expect to get out of the book, and/or what motivated the author to share the books contents with the world. **[see Exhibit I]**

The pages in-between

The *Pages in-between* come after the Introduction and includes chapters, sections, or categories. The chapters should be in the exact same order as the Table of Contents. In most cases the inside pages may be created first, and then the Table of Contents may be created to coincide with the inside contents and page numbers.

Page Numbers should be present throughout the book. They may be placed at the top or bottom, in the right or left corner; or the page numbers may be centered at the top or bottom of the pages. It is suggested that the *Author's Name* be placed either on every page or on every other page. Like the page numbers, the author's name may be placed at the top or bottom, in the right or left corner; or the author's name may be centered at the top or bottom of the pages. The placement of the page numbers and the author's name is completely the decision of the author and/or the publisher. **[see Exhibit J]**

The *title* of the book should be placed on every other page of the book. The title may be placed either at the top or bottom, on the right or left hand corner of the page, or the title may be centered at the top or bottom of the page. The pages in-between should include *Chapters* (or sections). It is suggested that the chapter always begin on an odd page number of the book and should be named with a Chapter title. The chapter title will be on the very first page of each Chapter, and should also be placed on every other page of the chapter, on the page opposite of the book title.

The final pages

There are several things that may be included on the final pages, after the chapters or sections. The writer may choose one or more of these options, but, all of them are not necessary.

The final pages may include:

An about the author section

Other books or products created by the author

Future works by the author

Other resources

Contact information

A Glossary

or an Index

About the author section

This section is about the author. It can be written by the author, but, expressed in the third party (as if someone else is saying it) and may include a photograph of the author. This section includes information such as the author's full name, age/birthday (optional), city and/or state of birth, basic family information. It is not suggested that personal family information be shared.

The section may also include background information about the author such as how the author grew up, past struggles that the author has overcome, where the author's knowledge and motivation to write the book came from (i.e. education, life or work experiences). While there is no limit to what the author may include in the About the Author section, it is suggested that the author <u>not</u> get too personal or discuss information that feels uncomfortable.

It is also suggested that the author include nothing that may be considered offensive or harmful to the readers or the author's family and friends. If there is a chance that someone could become offended or get hurt by something then it is suggested that the author refrain from including it in the book. It is further suggested that the author refrain from sharing information that is too intimate or sensitive with readers, especially if this is the author's first book. **[see Exhibit K1]**

Other books or products section

This page is totally optional. If the author has created or produced other books or products before their book was written then they can be included on pages after the About the Author section. **[see Exhibit K2]**

Future works by the author

If the author has new work(s) in progress that are expected to be published very soon after the book is complete, then the work(s) may be introduced to the readers on this page. This gives the readers something that they can look forward to.

Other resources

This section may include specific resources such as websites, addresses, and/or names of organizations that the author used to research information for their book. It may also include books read by other authors on similar subjects that the author feels would inspire or encourage the readers of their book. This section may also include a *bibliography* or a list of *references*. A *Bibliography* or *References* is a list of publications used by the author to find information to be used to support the views and opinions expressed by the author in the author's own book. **[see Exhibits K3]**

Contact information

Contact information for the publisher should be placed on the copyright page at the beginning of the book. However, contact information for the author may be placed at the end of the book as a way to specifically tell the readers how to order more copies of the book. It may also be used to invite the reader to write to the author to ask any questions, to express their comments or concerns, or to share a testimony of how the book affected them. This section may also used to tell readers how to book the author for speaking engagements, workshops, or conferences. **[see Exhibit K4]**

Glossary

A *glossary* is a list of terms, usually listed in alphabetical order, and display the dictionary meaning of the term. The glossary may also be used for the author to explain the context in which certain words were used in their book. **[see Exhibit K5]**

Index

An *index* is an alphabetical listing of certain items found in the book with page numbers of where to find the items. An index is similar to the table of context, but, has more detail. **[see Exhibit K6]**

YOUR ISBN, BAR CODE, AND PRE-ASSIGNED CONTROL NUMBER

6   Your ISBN

The letters ISBN stand for *International Standard Book Number*. Getting an ISBN is the key to making your book available to the world. The ISBN is a 13-digit number purchased through www.bowkerlink.com.

A publisher may purchase a minimum of one (1) ISBN at a time, up to a maximum of one thousand (1000). One ISBN should be used for the first book title published and one ISBN should be used for each book title published. This number identifies your book and belongs only to the title that you have assigned it to. At the time of this revision, one ISBN cost $125, ten ISBNs cost $250, one hundred ISBNs cost $575, and one thousand ISBNs cost $1000.

As soon as an ISBN is assigned to a book, the next step is to register the title with **Books-in-print** through www.bowkerlink.com. Books-in-print is a listing of every book published *and* in print. Bookstores, libraries, and retail outlets can find every published book, including the name, address and phone number of the publisher that published the book. Both publishers and retailers must register, be approved, and have a password to enter into the books-in-print portion of the website; and so while bookstores, libraries, and retail outlets have access to all of these books, access is not given to everyone.

Once your book title (and its assigned ISBN) is registered with Books-in-print it can be located by bookstores, libraries, and retail outlets. Furthermore, once you assign an ISBN to your book and register it with Books-in-print, anyone, anywhere who wants to purchase your book can walk into any bookstore, in any state, and give the ISBN, the title, or the author's name, and the bookstore will be able to search the Books-in-print database to find out how to order your book in order to sale it to customers.

When an ISBN is assigned to a book, the number should be preceded by the letters "ISBN" and placed on the copyright page of the book and on the bottom of the back cover of the book. The ISBN may be printed by itself or it may be embedded into a *Bar Code*.

7 Your Bar Code

A barcode is a group of vertical lines, usually black and white in color. It is printed on the back cover of the book at the bottom. In addition to the ISBN, the price may also be embedded into the barcode. When the ISBN and the price is embedded into the barcode, then bookstores and retail outlets can scan your book and the book information will automatically be put into their computer. Once the book information is in the computer, it comes up automatically when the cashier scans the barcode in order to ring it up for the customer to pay for it. Overall, a barcode makes it easier for bookstores and distributors to keep track of inventory, which results in more effective distribution and sale of your book. **[see Exhibit L for a sample of a barcode with the ISBN and the price embedded in it:]** You may purchase a bar code online at www.bowkerlink.com or your printer may provide one for you at the time of printing for an additional fee. Your printer will be the place that will print your bar code onto your books regardless of where you purchase the barcode. Your printer will also be the place that will embed your ISBN and price into your bar code.

8 Your Pre-assigned Control Number

Before publishing your book you may choose to apply for a *Pre-assigned Control Number*. This is a ten-digit number that is assigned to your book title by the Library of Congress before it is published. The purpose of the Pre-assigned Control Number (PCN) program is to save time for libraries. If a book is chosen to be placed in libraries, the libraries do not have to assign a control number to the book because the publisher has already done it through the Pre-assigned Control Number program. According to the Library of Congress "the publisher prints the control number in the book and thereby facilitates cataloging and other book processing activities." The Pre-assigned Control Number should be printed on the copyright page of your book in the following format:

Library of Congress Control Number 1234567890

To apply for a Pre-assigned Control Number or to learn more about the qualifications to receive one go to www.pcn.loc.gov .

PRINTING, DISTRIBUTING, AND MARKETING YOUR BOOK

For a book to be considered "published" it needs an ISBN <u>and</u> it needs to be listed with Books-in-print. These two things are what make your book available to the world. However, for the world to be able to actually purchase a copy of your book you must, first of all, have plenty of copies *printed* and available, and you must seek out a *distributor* to carry your book. Lastly, you must apply some *marketing* techniques.

9 | Printing Your Book

Digital printing -vs- Offset printing

Digital printing is done using the computer or a scanner and a printer. With digital printing your book is printed directly from the computer to a printer that is equipped to print books. The book pages may also be scanned into the digital printer and then printed. Digital printers are usually able to print as little as one book and so a publisher does not have to print large quantities in order for a digital printer to accept the job. Furthermore, digital printers will likely charge less than an offset printer for smaller quantities of books printed.

Offset printing is done by creating plates or films of the book and using large printing machines, not a computer and a printer, to make copies of the book. Offset printers usually charge a large "set-up" fee just to create the plates or films. So, it is not worth it to only get one book or only a small number of books printed by an offset printer. Offset printing becomes less expensive than digital printing when the publisher needs a very large number of books (2,000 or 3,000 or more). Regardless of whether digital or offset printing is used, the total cost of printing depends on the number of pages, ink color, and the quality of paper chosen for the inside pages and the book cover.

When requesting printing quotes, remember to ask about pricing for "perfect binding". If you are not familiar with paper quality, you may request pricing on a 10 pt or 12 pt, CS1 cover. CS1 means the cover is glossy on one side. For the inside pages you may request pricing on 50lb off-white paper. This is just to give you a place to begin. Be sure to go to the printing company and examine these items to be sure that they are the quality and color that you desire.

Print on Demand

Print on Demand is an alternative method to printing numerous copies of your book at the time of publication. It gives you the option of having your book printed in smaller quantities. You will benefit from print on demand if you cannot afford to order a large amount of books when you first publish your book. It allows you to print copies of your at the time you need them, or at the time a customer orders it. In some cases print on demand companies can mail the book(s) directly to your customer, making it appear as though the shipment is coming directly from you. This process is known as "drop shipping". With *Print on Demand*, you will pay more per copy of your printed book, but, it decreases your chances of ending up with a lot of unsold books sitting around in boxes.

There are numerous companies that offer Print on Demand services. Here are three that I am aware of: LULU.com, BookMasters, CreateSpace. I have never personally used these companies, so, I cannot attest to the quality of their service, good or bad. For more information about Print on Demand, I suggest conducting an online search for Print on Demand book printers and publishers.

10 Distributing Your Book

Most bookstores will not agree to carry your book unless it is distributed by a distributor that the bookstore orders from on a regular basis. This is because it cost too much money for bookstores to order one book title from one publisher, then another book title from another publisher. It is a lot easier for bookstores to order 100 different book titles from one distributor than to order 100 different book titles from 100 different publishers.

Three places to seek immediate distribution of your book are:

www.amazon.com (same as www.bordersbooks.com)
www.barnesandnoble.com
Baker and Taylor

Amazon.com and Barnesandnoble.com are websites that distribute the books that they sale through their websites. Bordersbooks.com has partnered with Amazon.com and so they are the exact same website. Books are sold through these websites when customers log on to the websites and shop and pay online. Amazon.com offers two programs for making your book available for purchase on their website: Advantage Program and Marketplace Program. With the Advantage program, Amazon.com will ship your book to the purchaser and provide full customer service. You pay a low annual fee and Amazon.com receives a large commission for selling your book. With the Marketplace program, <u>you</u> ship the book to the purchaser and <u>you</u> provide full customer service. Amazon.com receives a small amount per sale plus a small commission for selling your book. For more information about the Advantage program and the Marketplace program you may go online to <u>www.amazon.com</u>.

Baker and Taylor is a book wholesaler that distributes to bookstores, libraries, and various other retail outlets all over the United States. They are the second largest book wholesaler in the world. While many large distributors only distribute books for publishers who have published 10 or more books, Baker and Taylor has developed a program to distribute books for publishers who have published as little as only 1 book. For a fee, Baker and Taylor will even advertise the books that they distribute in one or more of their monthly or quarterly publications. For more information about partnering with Baker and Taylor go online to <u>www.btol.com</u>. If your book is accepted for distribution by Baker and Taylor, it may automatically be listed with Amazon.com at no cost to you and it would not be necessary for you to participate in Amazon.com's Advantage or Marketplace programs.

11 Marketing Your Book

People have a tendency to ask authors, how is your book doing? Well, the *book* is not doing anything, it is only a thing…it can't move. Books do not sale themselves, you must do some things to let the world know that your book is available and that they need your book, and you must also tell them *why* they need your book.

The responsibility for marketing your book is totally the job of the author and/or publisher. The author may take on the job of marketing the book themselves or a public relations specialist may be hired to publicize and market the book on the author's behalf.

Some of the techniques used in book marketing are:

Radio appearances

Radio commercials

Television appearances

Television commercials

Newspaper advertisements

Newspaper book reviews

Magazine book reviews

Speaking engagements

Vendor booths

Book signings

Online social media websites (i.e. Facebook, Twitter, etc.)

This book does not expound on marketing techniques. However, the way you market your book will be very important after your book is published. (Section 13 of this book offers some valuable resources for writers that will assist you in marketing your book)

12 | SELF-PUBLISHING YOUR E-BOOK

Times have changed and so have publishing. Over the past few years, more publishers are publishing e-books in addition to, or instead of, the hard copy. Why, most people are looking to save two things: time and money. E-book publishers save time because they do not have to go through the process of having the book printed and waiting for them to be shipped. They save money because they do not have to pay printing cost!

This section will answer the following questions:
- What is an e-book?
- Who buys e-books and why?
- What are the benefits of publishing an e-book?
- What does it cost to publish an e-book?
- How can I publish an e-book?
- What are the effects of e-books on the sale of hard copies?

What is an e-book?

An e-book is an electronic version of the paperback or hardback copy of your book. An e-book can be downloaded from an online website onto a variety of handheld e-Reader devices, like the Apple iPad, Barnes & Noble NOOK, Amazon KINDLE, and your home computer.

Who buys e-books and why?

Who buys e-books? Everyone! Readers learn of new ways to purchase e-books every day. Why? Because they are usually less expensive than the hard copy; readers can download their purchased book immediately as opposed to waiting for the hard copy to be shipped in the mail. Also, e-books allow readers to carry around tens, hundreds, and even thousands of books in their handheld e-Reader device. This decreases, and sometimes eliminates, the use of book bags and brief cases. So, travelers can carry numerous books on the bus or airplane without having to carry a bulky bag.

I recently learned that many libraries are slowly moving towards purchasing e-books, in lieu of hard copies, for their libraries. By purchasing an e-book, in lieu of a hard copy, librarians are able share one copy of the book with their other library branches with just a click of their computer mouse. Purchasing e-books allows libraries to use less shelf space because the books are stored on their computer. It decreases the chance of a library book becoming lost or stolen. It also ensures borrowers will return the book, since they are only allowed to borrow/download it for two weeks at a time; then the e-book is automatically freed up so another library customer can download and read it.

What are the benefits of publishing an e-book?

The benefits to publishing an e-book are as follows:
- You don't have to keep an inventory of books in your home living space
- You don't have to ship books to customers
- Your e-book becomes available to readers all over the world immediately after they purchase

What does it cost to publish an e-book?

Many e-book publishing companies offer free e-book publishing and distribution. These companies allow you to design your e-book and cover on their website, determine the cost of your e-book, and then make it available for purchase to their numerous e-book purchasers. The catch is that they earn a percentage of every copy of your e-book that is purchased and downloaded from their online website. However, in some cases, it may be necessary to hire a professional who has experience designing and uploading books to e-book publishing sites. The cost would depend entirely on the rate of the professional who is doing the work.

How can I publish an e-book?

Today, the two top publishers and sellers of e-books are:
- Barnesandnoble.com
- Amazon.com

Lulu.com is another example of free e-book publisher/distributor.

What are the effects of e-books on the sale of hard copies?

At this time, the sale of hard copies has not suffered because of e-book publication. This is because many readers still enjoy turning pages as they relax and read their book. Also, many e-book readers will purchase the hard copy in addition to the e-book for the same title.

13 RESOURCES FOR WRITERS

The Christian Writers' Market Guide, by Sally Stuart.

Jumpstart Your Book Sales, by Tom and Marilyn Ross

1001 Ways to Market Your Books, by John Kremer

Sell Your Book on Amazon, by Brent Sampson (foreword by Dan Poynter)

Song Writer's Market, by Writer's Digest Books

How To Pitch and Promote Your Songs, by Fred Koller

Speak and Grow Rich, by Dottie Walters and Lillie Walters

1001 Ways to Make More Money as a Speaker, Consultant or Trainer by Lilly Walters

14 OTHER HELPFUL RESOURCES

To register a copyright
Library of Congress
U. S. Copyright Office
101 Independence Avenue, S.E.
Washington, D.C. 20559-6000
Website: www.copyright.gov
(202) 707-3000

To obtain an ISBN
ISBN U.S. Agency
R.R. Bowker
630 Central Avenue
New Providence, NJ 07974
e-mail: isbn-san@bowker.com

To get your book on Barnesandnoble.com
Barnes & Noble Distribution Center
Attn: Merch Dept./New Vendor Processing
100 Middlesex Center Blvd.
Jamesburg, NJ 08831

Retail store placement with Barnes and Noble
If you would like your title to be considered for placement in Barnes & Noble stores, please submit a copy of the book (no manuscripts, please), along with marketing and promotion plans, trade reviews, and a note describing what makes the book unique, to:
The Small Press Department
Barnes & Noble, Inc.
122 Fifth Ave
New York, NY 10011
E-mail: btinfo@btol.com
1-800-775-1800

15   HELPFUL WEBSITES

To get your books listed with Books-in-print
www.bowkerlink.com

To obtain a Bar Code
www.bowkerlink.com

To obtain a Pre-assigned Control Number
http://pcn.loc.gov

To find a printer
www.printellectual.com

To get your book listed with Amazon.com and Borders.com
www.amazon.com

To get your book distributed by Baker & Taylor
www.btol.com

EXHIBITS - A through P

Exhibit A	Copyright Application – Long Form TX with instructions		43-46
Exhibit B	Copyright Application – Short Form TX with instructions		47-48
Exhibit C	Front Cover	49	
Exhibit D	Back Cover	50	
Exhibit E	Spine	51	
Exhibit F	Title Page	52	
Exhibit G	Copyright Page	53	
Exhibit H1	Acknowledgments	54	
Exhibit H2	Dedication	54	
Exhibit H3	Testimonials	55	
Exhibit H4	Preface	56	
Exhibit H5	Foreword	57	
Exhibit H6	Table of Contents	58	
Exhibit I	Introduction Page	59	
Exhibit J	Inside Pages - page numbers, author's name, book title	60	
Exhibit K1	About the Author	61	
Exhibit K2	Other Books and Products	62	
Exhibit K3	Bibliography/References	63	
Exhibit K4	Contact Information	64	
Exhibit L	Bar Code	65	

Writer's Breakthrough: *Steps to Copyright and Publish Your Own Book* Grace LaJoy Henderson

 Form TX

Detach and read these instructions before completing this form.
Make sure all applicable spaces have been filled in before you return this form.

Exhibit A
Copyright Application
(Pages 43-46)
Form TX Long Form
with Instructions

BASIC INFORMATION

When to Use This Form: Use Form TX for registration of published or unpublished nondramatic literary works, excluding periodicals or serial issues. This class includes a wide variety of works: fiction, nonfiction, poetry, textbooks, reference works, directories, catalogs, advertising copy, compilations of information, and computer programs. For periodicals and serials, use Form SE.

Deposit to Accompany Application: An application for copyright registration must be accompanied by a deposit consisting of copies or phonorecords representing the entire work for which registration is to be made. The following are the general deposit requirements as set forth in the statute:
   Unpublished Work: Deposit one complete copy (or phonorecord)
   Published Work: Deposit two complete copies (or one phonorecord) of the best edition.
   Work First Published Outside the United States: Deposit one complete copy (or phonorecord) of the first foreign edition.
   Contribution to a Collective Work: Deposit one complete copy (or phonorecord) of the best edition of the collective work.
   The Copyright Notice: Before March 1, 1989, the use of copyright notice was mandatory on all published works, and any work first published before that date should have carried a notice. For works first published on and after March 1, 1989, use of the copyright notice is optional. For more information about copyright notice, see Circular 3, *Copyright Notice.*

For Further Information: To speak to a Copyright Office staff member, call (202) 707-3000 or 1-877-476-0778 (toll free). Recorded information is available 24 hours a day. Order forms and other publications from the address in space 9 or call the Forms and Publications Hotline at (202) 707-9100. Access and download circulars, certain forms, and other information from the Copyright Office website at *www.copyright.gov.*

PRIVACY ACT ADVISORY STATEMENT Required by the Privacy Act of 1974 (P.L. 93-579)
The authority for requesting this information is title 17 U.S.C. §409 and §410. Furnishing the requested information is voluntary. But if the information is not furnished, it may be necessary to delay or refuse registration and you may not be entitled to certain relief, remedies, and benefits provided in chapters 4 and 5 of title 17 U.S.C
The principal uses of the requested information are the establishment and maintenance of a public record and the examination of the application for compliance with the registration requirements of the copyright code.
Other routine uses include public inspection and copying, preparation of public indexes, preparation of public catalogs of copyright registrations, and preparation of search reports upon request
NOTE: No other advisory statement will be given in connection with this application. Please keep this statement and refer to it if we communicate with you regarding this application

LINE-BY-LINE INSTRUCTIONS

Please type or print using black ink. The form is used to produce the certificate.

SPACE 1: Title

Title of This Work: Every work submitted for copyright registration must be given a title to identify that particular work. If the copies or phonorecords of the work bear a title or an identifying phrase that could serve as a title, transcribe that wording *completely* and *exactly* on the application. Indexing of the registration and future identification of the work will depend on the information you give here.

Previous or Alternative Titles: Complete this space if there are any additional titles for the work under which someone searching for the registration might be likely to look or under which a document pertaining to the work might be recorded.

Publication as a Contribution: If the work being registered is a contribution to a periodical, serial, or collection, give the title of the contribution in the "Title of This Work" space. Then, in the line headed "Publication as a Contribution," give information about the collective work in which the contribution appeared.

SPACE 2: Author(s)

General Instructions: After reading these instructions, decide who are the "authors" of this work for copyright purposes. Then, unless the work is a "collective work," give the requested information about every "author" who contributed any appreciable amount of copyrightable matter to this version of the work. If you need further space, request Continuation Sheets. In the case of a collective work, such as an anthology, collection of essays, or encyclopedia, give information about the author of the collective work as a whole.

Name of Author: The fullest form of the author's name should be given. Unless the work was "made for hire," the individual who actually created the work is its "author." In the case of a work made for hire, the statute provides that "the employer or other person for whom the work was prepared is considered the author."

What Is a "Work Made for Hire"? A "work made for hire" is defined as (1) "a work prepared by an employee within the scope of his or her employment"; or (2) "a work specially ordered or commissioned for use as a contribution to a collective work, as a part of a motion picture or other audiovisual work, as a translation, as a supplementary work, as a compilation, as an instructional text, as a test, as answer material for a test, or as an atlas, if the parties expressly agree in a written instrument signed by them that the works shall be considered a work made for hire." If you have checked "Yes" to indicate that the work was "made for hire," you must give the full legal name of the employer (or other person for whom the work was prepared). You may also include the name of the employee along with the name of the employer (for example: "Elster Publishing Co., employer for hire of John Ferguson").

"Anonymous" or "Pseudonymous" Work: An author's contribution to a work is "anonymous" if that author is not identified on the copies or phonorecords of the work. An author's contribution to a work is "pseudonymous" if that author is identified on the copies or phonorecords under a fictitious name. If the work is "anonymous" you may: (1) leave the line blank; or (2) state "anonymous" on the line; or (3) reveal the author's identity. If the work is "pseudonymous" you may: (1) leave the line blank; or (2) give the pseudonym and identify it as such (for example: "Huntley Haverstock, pseudonym"); or (3) reveal the author's name, making clear which is the real name and which is the pseudonym (for example, "Judith Barton, whose pseudonym is Madeline Elster"). However, the citizenship or domicile of the author *must* be given in all cases.

Dates of Birth and Death: If the author is dead, the statute requires that the year of death be included in the application unless the work is anonymous or pseudonymous. The author's birth date is optional but is

---

This form is from the U.S. Copyright Office website at www.copyright.gov

useful as a form of identification. Leave this space blank if the author's contribution was a "work made for hire."

Author's Nationality or Domicile: Give the country of which the author is a citizen or the country in which the author is domiciled. Nationality or domicile *must* be given in all cases.

Nature of Authorship: After the words "Nature of Authorship," give a brief general statement of the nature of this particular author's contribution to the work. Examples: "Entire text"; "Coauthor of entire text"; "Computer program"; "Editorial revisions"; "Compilation and English translation"; "New text."

SPACE 3: Creation and Publication

General Instructions: Do not confuse "creation" with "publication." Every application for copyright registration must state "the year in which creation of the work was completed." Give the date and nation of first publication only if the work has been published.

Creation: Under the statute, a work is "created" when it is fixed in a copy or phonorecord for the first time. Where a work has been prepared over a period of time, the part of the work existing in fixed form on a particular date constitutes the created work on that date. The date you give here should be the year in which the author completed the particular version for which registration is now being sought, even if other versions exist or if further changes or additions are planned.

Publication: The statute defines "publication" as "the distribution of copies or phonorecords of a work to the public by sale or other transfer of ownership, or by rental, lease, or lending." A work is also "published" if there has been an "offering to distribute copies or phonorecords to a group of persons for purposes of further distribution, public performance, or public display." Give the full date (month, day, year) when, and the country where, publication first occurred. If first publication took place simultaneously in the United States and other countries, it is sufficient to state "U.S.A."

SPACE 4: Claimant(s)

Name(s) and Address(es) of Copyright Claimant(s): Give the name(s) and address(es) of the copyright claimant(s) in this work even if the claimant is the same as the author. Copyright in a work belongs initially to the author of the work (including, in the case of a work made for hire, the employer or other person for whom the work was prepared). The copyright claimant is either the author of the work or a person or organization to whom the copyright initially belonging to the author has been transferred.

Transfer: The statute provides that, if the copyright claimant is not the author, the application for registration must contain "a brief statement of how the claimant obtained ownership of the copyright." If any copyright claimant named in space 4 is not an author named in space 2, give a brief statement explaining how the claimant(s) obtained ownership of the copyright. Examples: "By written contract"; "Transfer of all rights by author"; "Assignment"; "By will." Do not attach transfer documents or other attachments or riders.

SPACE 5: Previous Registration

General Instructions: The questions in space 5 are intended to show whether an earlier registration has been made for this work and, if so, whether there is any basis for a new registration. As a general rule, only one basic copyright registration can be made for the same version of a particular work.

Same Version: If this version is substantially the same as the work covered by a previous registration, a second registration is not generally possible unless: (1) the work has been registered in unpublished form and a second registration is now being sought to cover this first published edition; or (2) someone other than the author is identified as copyright claimant in the earlier registration, and the author is now seeking registration in his or her own name. If either of these two exceptions applies, check the appropriate box and give the earlier registration number and date. Otherwise, do not submit Form TX. Instead, write the Copyright Office for information about supplementary registration or recordation of transfers of copyright ownership.

Changed Version: If the work has been changed and you are now seeking registration to cover the additions or revisions, check the last box in space 5, give the earlier registration number and date, and complete both parts of space 6 in accordance with the instructions below.

Previous Registration Number and Date: If more than one previous registration has been made for the work, give the number and date of the latest registration.

SPACE 6: Derivative Work or Compilation

General Instructions: Complete space 6 if this work is a "changed version," "compilation," or "derivative work" and if it incorporates one or more earlier works that have already been published or registered for copyright or that have fallen into the public domain. A "compilation" is defined as "a work formed by the collection and assembling of preexisting materials or of data that are selected, coordinated, or arranged in such a way that the resulting work as a whole constitutes an original work of authorship." A "derivative work" is "a work based on one or more preexisting works." Examples of derivative works include translations, fictionalizations, abridgments, condensations, or "any other form in which a work may be recast, transformed, or adapted." Derivative works also include works "consisting of editorial revisions, annotations, or other modifications" if these changes, as a whole, represent an original work of authorship.

Preexisting Material (space 6a): For derivative works, complete this space *and* space 6b. In space 6a identify the preexisting work that has been recast, transformed, or adapted. The preexisting work may be material that has been previously published, previously registered, or that is in the public domain. An example of preexisting material might be: "Russian version of Goncharov's 'Oblomov.'"

Material Added to This Work (space 6b): Give a brief, general statement of the new material covered by the copyright claim for which registration is sought. *Derivative work* examples include: "Foreword, editing, critical annotations"; "Translation"; "Chapters 11–17." If the work is a *compilation*, describe both the compilation itself and the material that has been compiled. Example: "Compilation of certain 1917 speeches by Woodrow Wilson." A work may be both a derivative work and compilation, in which case a sample statement might be: "Compilation and additional new material."

SPACE 7, 8, 9: Fee, Correspondence, Certification, Return Address

Deposit Account: If you maintain a Deposit Account in the Copyright Office, identify it in space 7a. Otherwise leave the space blank and send the fee with your application and deposit.

Correspondence (space 7b): Give the name, address, area code, telephone number, fax number, and email address (if available) of the person to be consulted if correspondence about this application becomes necessary.

Certification (space 8): The application cannot be accepted unless it bears the date and the *handwritten signature* of the author or other copyright claimant, or of the owner of exclusive right(s), or of the duly authorized agent of author, claimant, or owner of exclusive right(s).

Address for Return of Certificate (space 9): The address box must be completed legibly because the certificate will be returned in a window envelope.

This form is from the U.S. Copyright Office website at www.copyright.gov

> **Exhibit A**
> continued

Form TX
For a Nondramatic Literary Work
UNITED STATES COPYRIGHT OFFICE
REGISTRATION NUMBER

_____

TX   TXU
EFFECTIVE DATE OF REGISTRATION

_____
Month   Day   Year

Copyright Office fees are subject to change. For current fees, check the Copyright Office website at www.copyright.gov, write the Copyright Office, or call (202) 707-3000.

Privacy Act Notice: Sections 408-410 of title 17 of the *United States Code* authorize the Copyright Office to collect the personally identifying information requested on this form in order to process the application for copyright registration. By providing this information you are agreeing to routine uses of the information that include publication to give legal notice of your copyright claim as required by 17 U.S.C. §705. It will appear in the Office's online catalog. If you do not provide the information requested, registration may be refused or delayed, and you may not be entitled to certain relief, remedies, and benefits under the copyright law.

DO NOT WRITE ABOVE THIS LINE. IF YOU NEED MORE SPACE, USE A SEPARATE CONTINUATION SHEET.

1 TITLE OF THIS WORK ▼

PREVIOUS OR ALTERNATIVE TITLES ▼

PUBLICATION AS A CONTRIBUTION If this work was published as a contribution to a periodical, serial, or collection, give information about the collective work in which the contribution appeared.   **Title of Collective Work** ▼

If published in a periodical or serial give: Volume ▼   Number ▼   Issue Date ▼   On Pages ▼

2 a NAME OF AUTHOR ▼   DATES OF BIRTH AND DEATH
                                                                                            Year Born ▼   Year Died ▼

Was this contribution to the work a   AUTHOR'S NATIONALITY OR DOMICILE   WAS THIS AUTHOR'S CONTRIBUTION TO
"work made for hire"?   Name of Country   THE WORK   If the answer to either
❑ Yes   OR { Citizen of _____   Anonymous?   ❑ Yes ❑ No   of these questions is
❑ No   Domiciled in _____   Pseudonymous? ❑ Yes ❑ No   "Yes," see detailed instructions.

NOTE
Under the law, the "author" of a "work made for hire" is generally the employer, not the employee (see instructions). For any part of this work that was "made for hire" check "Yes" in the space provided, give the employer (or other person for whom the work was prepared) as "Author" of that part, and leave the space for dates of birth and death blank.

NATURE OF AUTHORSHIP Briefly describe nature of material created by this author in which copyright is claimed. ▼

b NAME OF AUTHOR ▼   DATES OF BIRTH AND DEATH
                                                                                            Year Born ▼   Year Died ▼

Was this contribution to the work a   AUTHOR'S NATIONALITY OR DOMICILE   WAS THIS AUTHOR'S CONTRIBUTION TO
"work made for hire"?   Name of Country   THE WORK   If the answer to either
❑ Yes   OR { Citizen of _____   Anonymous?   ❑ Yes ❑ No   of these questions is
❑ No   Domiciled in _____   Pseudonymous? ❑ Yes ❑ No   "Yes," see detailed instructions.

NATURE OF AUTHORSHIP Briefly describe nature of material created by this author in which copyright is claimed. ▼

c NAME OF AUTHOR ▼   DATES OF BIRTH AND DEATH
                                                                                            Year Born ▼   Year Died ▼

Was this contribution to the work a   AUTHOR'S NATIONALITY OR DOMICILE   WAS THIS AUTHOR'S CONTRIBUTION TO
"work made for hire"?   Name of Country   THE WORK   If the answer to either
❑ Yes   OR { Citizen of _____   Anonymous?   ❑ Yes ❑ No   of these questions is
❑ No   Domiciled in _____   Pseudonymous? ❑ Yes ❑ No   "Yes," see detailed instructions.

NATURE OF AUTHORSHIP Briefly describe nature of material created by this author in which copyright is claimed. ▼

3 a YEAR IN WHICH CREATION OF THIS   **b** DATE AND NATION OF FIRST PUBLICATION OF THIS PARTICULAR WORK
       WORK WAS COMPLETED This information   Complete this information Month _____ Day _____ Year _____
                           must be given   ONLY if this work
                       Year in all cases.   has been published. _____ Nation

4 COPYRIGHT CLAIMANT(S) Name and address must be given even if the claimant is the same as   APPLICATION RECEIVED
       the author given in space 2. ▼   _____
                                                                                                   ONE DEPOSIT RECEIVED
                                                                                                   _____
See instructions   TWO DEPOSITS RECEIVED
before completing   _____
this space.   TRANSFER If the claimant(s) named here in space 4 is (are) different from the author(s) named in   FUNDS RECEIVED
                  space 2, give a brief statement of how the claimant(s) obtained ownership of the copyright. ▼   _____

MORE ON BACK ▶ • Complete all applicable spaces (numbers 5-9) on the reverse side of this page.   DO NOT WRITE HERE
                • See detailed instructions.   • Sign the form at line 8.   Page 1 of ____ pages

---

This form is from the U.S. Copyright Office website at www.copyright.gov

Writer's Breakthrough: *Steps to Copyright and Publish Your Own Book*   Grace LaJoy Henderson

Exhibit A continued

EXAMINED BY _____	FORM TX
CHECKED BY _____	
☐ CORRESPONDENCE Yes	FOR COPYRIGHT OFFICE USE ONLY

DO NOT WRITE ABOVE THIS LINE. IF YOU NEED MORE SPACE, USE A SEPARATE CONTINUATION SHEET.

PREVIOUS REGISTRATION Has registration for this work, or for an earlier version of this work, already been made in the Copyright Office?
☐ Yes ☐ No If your answer is "Yes," why is another registration being sought? (Check appropriate box.) ▼
a. ☐ This is the first published edition of a work previously registered in unpublished form.
b. ☐ This is the first application submitted by this author as copyright claimant.
c. ☐ This is a changed version of the work, as shown by space 6 on this application.
If your answer is "Yes," give: **Previous Registration Number** ▶   **Year of Registration** ▶

5

DERIVATIVE WORK OR COMPILATION
Preexisting Material Identify any preexisting work or works that this work is based on or incorporates. ▼

Material Added to This Work Give a brief, general statement of the material that has been added to this work and in which copyright is claimed. ▼

6 a b
See instructions before completing this space.

DEPOSIT ACCOUNT If the registration fee is to be charged to a deposit account established in the Copyright Office, give name and number of account.
Name ▼   **Account Number** ▼

CORRESPONDENCE Give name and address to which correspondence about this application should be sent. Name/Address/Apt/City/State/Zip ▼

Area code and daytime telephone number ▶   Fax number ▶
Email ▶

7 a b

CERTIFICATION* I, the undersigned, hereby certify that I am the
Check only one ▶
☐ author
☐ other copyright claimant
☐ owner of exclusive right(s)
☐ authorized agent of _____
Name of author or other copyright claimant, or owner of exclusive right(s) ▲
of the work identified in this application and that the statements made by me in this application are correct to the best of my knowledge.

8

Typed or printed name and date ▼ If this application gives a date of publication in space 3, do not sign and submit it before that date.
_____ Date ▶ _____

Handwritten signature ▼

Certificate will be mailed in window envelope to this address:

Name ▼
Number/Street/Apt ▼
City/State/Zip ▼

YOU MUST:
• Complete all necessary spaces
• Sign your application in space 8
SEND ALL 3 ELEMENTS IN THE SAME PACKAGE:
1. Application form
2. Nonrefundable filing fee in check or money order payable to Register of Copyrights
3. Deposit material
MAIL TO:
Library of Congress
Copyright Office-TX
101 Independence Avenue SE
Washington, DC 20559

9

*17 U.S.C. §506(e): Any person who knowingly makes a false representation of a material fact in the application for copyright registration provided for by section 409, or in any written statement filed in connection with the application, shall be fined not more than $2,500.

Form TX—Full Reviewed: 07/2012 Printed on recycled paper   U.S. Government Printing Office: 2012-xxx-xxx/xx,xxx

This form is from the U.S. Copyright Office website at www.copyright.gov

> **Exhibit B - Copyright Application**
> (Pages 47-48)
> Form TX Short Form - *with Instructions*

Instructions for Short Form TX

For nondramatic literary works, including fiction and nonfiction, books, short stories, poems, collections of poetry, essays, articles in serials, and computer programs

USE THIS FORM IF —
1. You are the *only* author and copyright owner of this work, *and*
2. The work was *not* made for hire, *and*
3. The work is completely new (does not contain a substantial amount of material that has been previously published or registered or is in the public domain).

If any of the above does not apply, you may register online at www.copyright.gov or use Form TX.

Note: *Short Form TX is not appropriate for an anonymous author who does not wish to reveal his or her identity.*

HOW TO COMPLETE SHORT FORM TX
- Type or print in black ink.
- Be clear and legible.
- Give only the information requested.

Note: You may use a continuation sheet (Form __/CON) to list individual titles in a collection. Complete Space A and list the individual titles under Space C on the back page. Space B is not applicable to short forms.

1 Title of This Work

You must give a title. If there is no title, state "UNTITLED." If you are registering an unpublished collection, give the collection title you want to appear in our records (for example: "Joan's Poems, Volume 1"). Alternative title: If the work is known by two titles, you also may give the second title. If the work has been published as part of a larger work (including a periodical), give the title of that larger work in addition to the title of the contribution.

2 Name and Address of Author and Owner of the Copyright

Give your name and mailing address. You may include your pseudonym followed by "pseud." Also, give the nation of which you are a citizen or where you have your domicile (i.e., permanent residence).
Give daytime phone and fax numbers and email address, if available.

3 Year of Creation

Give the latest year in which you completed the work you are registering at this time. A work is "created" when it is written down, stored in a computer, or otherwise "fixed" in a tangible form.

4 Publication

If the work has been published (i.e., if copies have been distributed to the public), give the complete date of publication (month, day, and year) and the nation where the publication first took place.

5 Type of Authorship in This Work

Check the box or boxes that describe your authorship in the copy you are sending with the application. For example, if you are registering a story and are planning to add illustrations later, check only the box for "text."

A "compilation" of terms or of data is a selection, coordination, or arrangement of such information into a chart, directory, or other form. A compilation of previously published or public domain material must be registered using a standard Form TX.

6 Signature of Author

Sign the application in black ink and check the appropriate box. The person signing the application should be the author or his/her authorized agent.

7 Person to Contact for Rights/Permissions

This space is optional. You may give the name and address of the person or organization to contact for permission to use the work. You may also provide phone, fax, or email information.

8 Certificate Will Be Mailed

This space must be completed. Your certificate of registration will be mailed in a window envelope to this address. Also, if the Copyright Office needs to contact you, we will write to this address.

9 Deposit Account

Complete this space only if you currently maintain a deposit account in the Copyright Office.

MAIL WITH THE FORM

- The filing fee in the form of a check or money order (*no cash*) payable to *Register of Copyrights*, and
- One or two copies of the work. If the work is unpublished, send one copy. If published, send two copies of the best published edition. (If first published outside the U.S., send one copy either as first published or of the best edition.) **Note:** Inquire about special requirements for works first published before 1978. Copies submitted become the property of the U.S. government.

Mail everything (application form, copy or copies, and fee) *in one package* to:
Library of Congress
Copyright Office-TX
101 Independence Avenue SE
Washington, DC 20559

QUESTIONS? Call (202) 707-3000 or 1-877-476-0778 (toll free) between 8:30 AM and 5:00 PM eastern time, Monday through Friday, except federal holidays. For forms and informational circulars, call (202) 707-9100 24 hours a day, 7 days a week. Download circulars and forms or register online at *www.copyright.gov*.

PRIVACY ACT ADVISORY STATEMENT Required by the Privacy Act of 1974 (P.L. 93-579)
The authority for requesting this information is title 17 U.S.C. §409 and §410. Furnishing the requested information is voluntary. But if the information is not furnished, it may be necessary to delay or refuse registration and you may not be entitled to certain relief, remedies, and benefits provided in chapters 4 and 5 of title 17 U.S.C.
The principal uses of the requested information are the establishment and maintenance of a public record and the examination of the application for compliance with the registration requirements of the copyright law.
Other routine uses include public inspection and copying, preparation of public indexes, preparation of public catalogs of copyright registrations, and preparation of search reports upon request.
NOTE: No other advisory statement will be given in connection with this application. Please keep this statement and refer to it if we communicate with you regarding this application.

> This form is from the U.S. Copyright Office website at www.copyright.gov

Writer's Breakthrough: *Steps to Copyright and Publish Your Own Book* — Grace LaJoy Henderson

**Exhibit B
continued**

Short Form TX
For a Nondramatic Literary Work
UNITED STATES COPYRIGHT OFFICE
REGISTRATION NUMBER

Copyright Office fees are subject to change. For current fees, check the Copyright Office website at www.copyright.gov, write the Copyright Office, or call (202) 707-3000 or 1-877-476-0778.

Privacy Act Notice: Sections 408-410 of title 17 of the *United States Code* authorize the Copyright Office to collect the personally identifying information requested on this form in order to process the application for copyright registration. By providing this information, you are agreeing to routine uses of the information that include publication to give legal notice of your copyright claim as required by 17 U.S.C. §705. It will appear in the Office's online catalog. If you do not provide the information requested, registration may be refused or delayed, and you may not be entitled to certain relief, remedies, and benefits under the copyright law.

TX   TXU
Effective Date of Registration

Application Received

Examined By

Deposit Received
One   Two

Correspondence
Fee Received

TYPE OR PRINT IN BLACK INK. DO NOT WRITE ABOVE THIS LINE.

1 Title of This Work:
Alternative title or title of larger work in which this work was published:

2 Name and Address of Author and Owner of the Copyright:
Nationality or domicile:
Phone, fax, and email:
Phone _____ Fax _____
Email _____

3 Year of Creation:

4 *If work has been published,* Date and Nation of Publication:
a. Date _____ Month _____ Day _____ Year _____ (Month, day, and year all required)
b. Nation

5 Type of Authorship in This Work:
Check all that this author created.
❏ Text (includes fiction, nonfiction, poetry, computer programs, etc.)
❏ Illustrations
❏ Photographs
❏ Compilation of terms or data

6 Signature:
Registration cannot be completed without a signature.
I certify that the statements made by me in this application are correct to the best of my knowledge. Check one:
❏ Author   ❏ Authorized agent
X _____

7 (OPTIONAL) Name and Address of Person to Contact for Rights and Permissions:
Phone, fax, and email:
❏ Check here if same as #2 above.
Phone _____ Fax _____
Email _____

8 Certificate will be mailed in window envelope to this address:
Name ▼
Number/Street/Apt ▼
City/State/Zip ▼

9 Deposit account # _____
Name _____
Complete this space only if you currently hold a Deposit Account in the Copyright Office.

DO NOT WRITE HERE   Page 1 of ___ pages

*17 U.S.C. § 506(e): Any person who knowingly makes a false representation of a material fact in the application for copyright registration provided for by section 409, or in any written statement filed in connection with the application, shall be fined not more than $2,500.

Form TX-Short   Rev: 02/2012   Printed on recycled paper   U.S. Government Printing Office: 2012-xxx-xxx/xx,xxx

This form is from the U.S. Copyright Office website at www.copyright.gov

Exhibit C
Front Cover

Dr. Grace LaJoy Henderson

A Gifted Child In Foster Care

A Story of Resilience

Exhibit D
Back Cover

> "Simply put, this book will help you LEARN MORE ABOUT YOUR STUDENT to HELP YOUR STUDENT LEARN."
>
> -Grace LaJoy, author
> A Gifted Child in Foster Care

Tapping into the Gifts and Talents of Special Education Students educates the educator about how tap into the lifeline of educating students with learning disabilities, through identifying their gifts, talents and learning styles, and using them to educate.

Regular and special educators will receive an overview of personal experiences, steps, and learning style inventories that will enhance their classroom teaching skills. This book will aide educators in reaching their full potential, by providing them with helpful tools to assist them in learning more about their students.

The tools in this book are designed to help teachers
- know and understand their students' learning style
- use their students' learning style to
  * enhance classroom learning
  * increase students' thinking and analytical skills

This book will guide teachers in:

- Identifying Leadership qualities in their students
- Enhancing communication and respect for their students
- Recognizing gifts and talents in students
- Encouraging students to develop their gifts and talents through the education process
- Knowing what signs to look for to determine if a student should be referred to the special education program.

Obtain copies of this book today! Use it as a vital tool for professional and educational development for all educators and students.

ISBN: 978-0-9829404-0-2

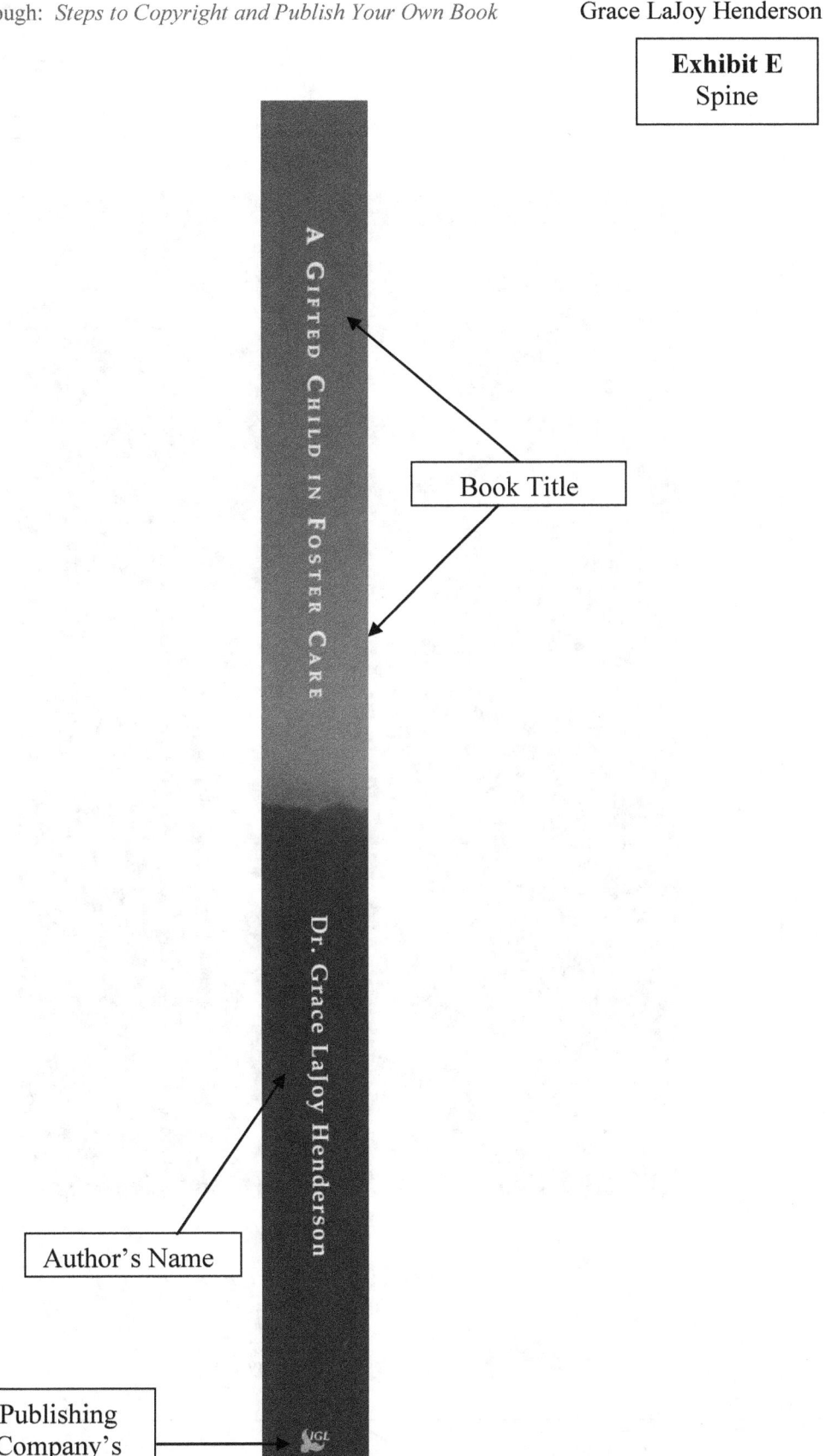

Publishing Company's Name and Logo

> **Exhibit G**
> **Copyright Page**

A Gifted Child
IN FOSTER CARE   *Dr. Grace LaJoy Henderson*

A GIFTED CHILD IN FOSTER CARE
Copyright ©2009. Grace LaJoy Henderson
Published by Inspirations by Grace LaJoy
Raymore, MO
www.gracelajoy.com

Library of Congress Control Number: 2009932965

ISBN 978-0-9814607-8-9

All rights reserved. No portion of this book may be copied, reproduced or transmitted in any form without prior written permission from the publisher.

Printed in the United States of America

A Gifted Child
IN FOSTER CARE

Dr. Grace LaJoy Henderson

> **Exhibit H2**
> Dedication

Dedication

My mother, Gloria Dawn Williams, who left me when I was two years old, never to return.

My father, James Thompson, who tried to keep his children together. He passed away on March 8, 1990.

My children Aric and Arica.

My siblings James D. Thompson, Gregory L. Thompson, Tyrone Thompson, Chrystal J. Thompson, and Darlene L. Thompson-Williams.

My sister-in-laws Paula R. Thompson and Sharon R. Thompson.

My foster parents, Willie and Pearlie Mae Wiggins, who offered me a stable home environment for three years.

Acknowledgments

> **Exhibit H1**
> Acknowledgments

Sugar Lee Lewis, who encouraged me to write this book.

Mark Littleton, for his editorial assistance.

Educators who noticed my gifts and creative talent, made me aware of it, and helped cultivate it.

A Gifted Child   Dr. Grace LaJoy Henderson
IN FOSTER CARE

More praise for
A GIFTED CHILD IN FOSTER CARE

"**A Gifted Child in Foster Care** is well written, inspiring, and has a beautiful message. It will encourage students in Gifted and Talented Programs to use their gifts."

~**Dr. Grace Ann Ancona**, Coordinator
Gifted and Talented Program
Kansas City Missouri School District

"This book paints a good picture of the basic needs of all children. It lets older youth know they can become someone."

~**Traci Wallin**, MSW,
Foster Care Program Manager
Catholic Charities – Kansas City

"A compelling story and great principles about working with children in foster care. Anyone who reads this will gain a better understanding of how to nurture and build children's lives toward success."

~**Mark Littleton, Th.M.**, Author
Big Bad God of the Bible

"Grace LaJoy's story is proof that when placed in a positive environment, including foster care, children can discover their potential. This book will benefit young adults in foster care and foster parents who have become frustrated with 'the system'. Readers will gain a greater understanding of foster care and what happens from a child's perspective."

~**Ann Graves**, Family Development Specialist
Catholic Charities Family Advocates

Continued →

> **Exhibit H4**
> Preface

PREFACE

There is a great need for writers to know how to copyright and publish their work. So many writers have poems, stories, and other types of writings just sitting in a drawer, in a box, or in a notebook. These gifted writers have written things that could positively change the hearts and minds of people all over the world, if only they knew the steps necessary to make their work available to the world. <u>Writer's Breakthrough</u> meets the need of the writer who has a book ready for publication, but does not know where to begin. It empowers the writer who feels overwhelmed with the high costs of self-publishing companies. It encourages the writer who has inquired about copyrighting and publishing but never seems to get all of the necessary answers. Now that <u>Writer's Breakthrough</u> is here, the beginning writer's search for specific answers is over!

A Gifted Child *Dr. Grace LaJoy Henderson*
IN FOSTER CARE

Foreword

Dr. Grace LaJoy has penned a touching and well-written chronicle of her childhood within a loving family that had to contend with poverty, mental illness, abandonment and other daunting challenges. No matter how tough things got, or the hurdles she faced, this strong and sensitive young woman never wavered in her drive to be successful.

Her trail blazing approach and single-minded struggle to achieve are a model for *all* children coming from difficult circumstances, not just the gifted. Her touching acknowledgement of the role of "Big mama," her foster mother, in her eventual success is a testament to all those foster parents who work tirelessly to change the world 'one child at a time.'

A Gifted Child in Foster Care instills values and encourages hard work and persistence, while addressing the great life challenges faced by children growing up in foster care. It is a great read for foster children, foster parents, caseworkers, CASA volunteers, and juvenile court judges.

~**Tom Kircher**
Director of Illinois Recruitment
Foster and Adoptive Care Coalition

A Gifted Child
IN FOSTER CARE

Dr. Grace LaJoy Henderson

Table of Contents

FOREWORD – DR. SUGAR LEE LEWIS		VIII
FOREWORD – TOM KIRCHER		IX
FOREWORD – PEARLIE MAE WIGGINS		X
INTRODUCTION		1
A WORD FROM THE AUTHOR		3
CHAPTER 1	LEFT BY MOTHER	7
CHAPTER 2	LIVING WITH DADDY	15
CHAPTER 3	GRANDMOTHER	19
CHAPTER 4	LEFT BY FATHER	25
CHAPTER 5	LIVING IN FOSTER CARE	29
CHAPTER 6	SEPARATED FROM SIBLINGS	37
CHAPTER 7	A TYPICAL DAY IN FOSTER CARE	43
CHAPTER 8	HOW FOSTER CARE SHAPED MY LIFE	49
CHAPTER 9	LIFE AFTER FOSTER CARE	53
CHAPTER 10	DADDY LEFT AGAIN	59
CHAPTER 11	PREGNANT AT SEVENTEEN	67
CHAPTER 12	MY GIFT REVEALED	75
CHAPTER 13	EMPOWERMENT FOR YOUTH	79
CHAPTER 14	EMPOWERMENT FOR PARENTS	83
POEM – "HE'S WORTH IT"		86
DISCUSSION TOPICS		88
GRACE LAJOY'S LIFE TIMELINE		93
GLOSSARY OF TERMS		97
INDEX		100

A Gifted Child Dr. Grace LaJoy Henderson
IN FOSTER CARE

Introduction

Over the years the words "foster child" and "foster care" often breed negative connotations. Children in foster care are often looked upon as not capable of succeeding in life. Children often leave foster care feeling mistreated or abused. **A Gifted Child in Foster Care** leaves the reader with a different, positive definition of "foster child" and "foster care."

In this book, Dr. Grace LaJoy shares her life story of being deserted by her mother, living in foster care, and ending up in a gifted and talented class while still in foster care. She recalls her life story before, during and after foster care. Her turbulent life experiences reveal how she became strong and began to encourage, inspire and empower others through her gift of writing.

Finally, she offers words of inspiration, encouragement, and empowerment to both children and parents. Children learn that they can succeed and impact the lives of others even in the face of adversity. Parents learn specific steps to help children recognize and utilize their gift(s).

A Gifted Child in Foster Care was developed as an

A Gifted Child
IN FOSTER CARE

Dr. Grace LaJoy Henderson

10 – Daddy Left Again

About two and a half years after my father got us out of foster care, he left us again! I was thirteen years old. *This time* he left my sisters and me to live with a lady in North Carolina. All three of my brothers had gone to the military by this time. This lady was not one of Daddy's girlfriends. She was simply an older lady who he entrusted to look out for us until we could find a place of our own, while he traveled looking for cement work.

Before Daddy left again, he gave my eighteen-year old sister, Chrystal, specific instructions about how to provide for me and Darlene without him. Chrystal found a townhome for us to live in that charged rent according to our income. Since we did not have any income, we paid nothing for rent.

"...my life was threatened when I was thirteen years old."

We moved into the townhome during my eighth grade year and I began riding the school bus to the junior high school. I met many children at school and in the townhome complex that I lived in. I also had many experiences, both good and bad, while living with my sisters. Of all the things that happened, the scariest experience was the time my life was threatened when I was thirteen years

Daddy Left Again   59

Tapping into the Gifts, Talents and Learning Styles of Special Education Students

Arlivia S. White, MA Sp.Ed.
Grace LaJoy Henderson, PhD

ABOUT THE AUTHORS

ARLIVIA S. WHITE, MA SP.ED.

Author, Speaker, and Workshop Presenter, Arlivia White has earned a Master's Degree in Special Education, and has over twenty years of service in the field of education. She has connected special education students and their families with resources to help them become successful in the classroom. She has also volunteered in her community for numerous years. When not in the classroom, this multi-talented singer and songwriter taps into her own gifts and talents. So, she is committed to compelling teachers to recognize student's gifts, talents, and learning styles, and begin incorporating them into classroom instruction.

GRACE LAJOY HENDERSON, PHD

Author, Inspirational Speaker and Workshop Facilitator, Dr. Grace LaJoy Henderson has earned a PhD in Christian Counseling and an undergraduate degree in Social Psychology. She has published a total of eighteen books; conducts author visits in schools; and has appeared in local and national news.

Her latest book is entitled, "A Gifted Child in Foster Care: A Story of Resilience", which comes with a matching Teacher's Guide and Student Workbook, is currently being used in classrooms throughout the United States. Her amazing story proves that even in the face of adversity, students can rise above their circumstances, recognize their strengths, and reach their goals. Her mission is to change the way children are viewed who live in diverse situations, such as foster care; and to magnify the fact that all children have a gift and the ability to be successful regardless of their background or circumstances.

36

> **Exhibit K2**
> Other Books and/or Products

Books and Resources Available by Dr. Grace LaJoy Henderson

A Gifted Child in Foster Care: *A Story of Resilience* (Book)

A Gifted Child in Foster Care: *Student Workbook*

A Gifted Child in Foster Care: *Teacher's Guide*

Tapping into the Gifts, Talents, and Learning Styles of Special Education Students (Book)

Understanding Each Other: *A Guide for Parents and their Children* (Book)

Sexual Purity and the Young Woman: *A Guide to Sexual Purity*
(A reference book for teen and college-age girls)

An Urgent Call to the Power of Ministry: *Realizing your ministry through your life experiences*

More Than Mere Words: *Poetry That Ministers* (Christian Poetry Book)

Diversity and my Credit Union: *A True Story* (Book)

My Automobile Dealership: *A True Story* (Book)

Writer's Breakthrough: *Steps to Copyright and Publish Your Own Book*
(Book and CD)

How Can Jesus Be God? (Children's Book)

Poetic Book Series
Diversity in our Schools
Diversity in our Workplace
The Bad Butt Kids
He's Worth It
Our Employees…Our Cornerstones

Poetic Empowerment (Spoken Word CD)

Songs by Grace LaJoy (Music CD)

To learn more please visit us online at www.gracelajoy.com

Exhibit K3
Bibliography/ References

Bibliography/References

Doe, John. <u>My Inheritance</u>. Charista House, 2009.

Henderson, Grace LaJoy. <u>More Than Mere Words</u>. IGL Publishing, 2009.

Doell, Janice. <u>You Are Special</u>. Wisemen Press, 2010.

Carallo, Stormy. <u>The Power of Life</u>. Harvet Publishers, 2010.

Smoke, Jamella. <u>Growing with the World</u>. Charista House, 2011.

Warrena, Maverick. <u>The Purpose of Life</u>. Banderman Press, 2012.

Exhibit K4
Contact Information

If you would like for Grace LaJoy Henderson to personally share what she has learned about book publishing with members of your group or organization you may contact her at:

Inspirations by Grace LaJoy
Post Office Box 181468
Arlington, TX 76096
E-mail: poetry@gracelajoy.com
Phone: (816) 318-1388

Exhibit L
Bar Code

This *Bar Code* with ISBN and Price embedded is from

Becoming Whole Before Becoming One

Sandra J. Scott, Author

(exact image of barcode used by permission)

Glossary

Bar Code – A group of vertical lines, usually black and white in color. It is printed on the back cover of the book at the bottom.

Books-in-print – A listing of every book published and in print.

Copyright – The right to copy a book that has been put into tangible format.

Distributor – The company that warehouses and ships book to retail outlets, schools, and libraries.

E-book – An electronic version of the paperback or hardback copy of your book. An e-book can be downloaded from an online website onto a variety of handheld e-Reader devices, like the Apple iPad, Barnes & Noble NOOK, Amazon KINDLE, and your home computer.

ISBN – *International Standard Book Number*. The ISBN is a 10-digit number purchased through www.bowkerlink.com. This number identifies a specific book and belongs only to the title that it is assigned it to.

Marketing – Techniques used to let the world know that a book is available, and to encourage consumers to purchase the book.

Pre-assigned Control Number – A ten-digit number that is assigned to your book title by the Library of Congress before it is published. The purpose of the Pre-assigned Control Number (PCN) program is to facilitate cataloging and other book processing activities if the book title is chosen to be included with the library holdings.

Printing – Reproducing multiple copies of a book.

Production – Designing a book and putting it into the most professional form possible in order to prepare it for consumer purchase.

Publish – To make your book available to the world.

Resource – A source of information, such as a book, a website, or an address that will assist writers in succeeding at their goal of publishing their book. (i.e. The Christian Writers Market, Bowkerlink.com, U.S. Library of Congress, etc.)

Self Publisher – A publishing company that publishes an author's book for a fee. The author retains all copyrights to the book.

Traditional Publisher – A publishing company that buys the rights to publish a book from an author. The publishing company pays all cost to publish, distribute, and market the book. The publishing company owns all copyrights to the book.

Writer's Breakthrough- A book designed to educate writers who know nothing about copyrighting and/or publishing their own book. A book that is short, simple, easy to read and to understand, as well as informative; a book that will motivate and encourage beginning writers to get started using your God-given writing talent immediately.

INDEX

About the author section	20,24,25,41,61
Acknowledgements	22,23,54
Amazon.com	30,21,34,39
Baker and Taylor	30,31,39
Bar Code	18,27,28,39,67
Barnesandnoble.com	30,34,38
Bibliography	26,41,63
Book, back cover	20-21,27,28,50
Book, cover	19
Book, front cover	19-21,49
Book, inside pages	21,23,29,60
Book, spine	19,21,51
Books-in-print	27,29,39,67
Bordersbooks.com	30,39
Contact information	24,27,64
Copyright application, long form	41,43-46
Copyright application, short form	41,47-48
Copyright, online	13
Copyright page	21,22,26-28,41
Copyright, poor man's	11,13
Copyright, register	12,67
Cover, front/back/spine	19,20,21
Dedications	22,41,54
Distributing your book	18,30
E-book	33-35,67
Final pages	21,24
Foreword	8,22,23,41,57
Future works by the author	24,25

Index continued

Glossary	24,26,67
Index	24,26,68,69
Inside pages	19,21,23,29,41,60
Introduction page	21,23,41,59
ISBN	2,18,21,22,27-29,38,65,67
Marketing	17,18,29,32,67
Other books or products section	24,25,41,62
Other resources	24,25
Page after the copyright page	21,22
Pages in-between	21,23,24
Pre-assigned Control Number	18,22,28,39,67
Preface	3,22,23,41,56
Print on Demand	30
Printing your book	18,29
Printing, digital/offset	29
Producing your book	18,19
Publish	3,17,18,67
Publishing, e-book	33-35
Publishing, self	17,67
Publishing, steps to	15,17,18
Publishing, traditional	17,18,67
References	26,41,63
Resources	17,24,25,32,37,38,70
Table of Contents	5,15,22,23,41,58
Testimonials	4,21-23,41,55
Title of book	20,21,24
Title page	21,22,41,52
U. S. Copyright Office	11-13,15,38
Websites	7,25,30,31,32,39

Other Books and Resources
by Dr. Grace LaJoy Henderson

A Gifted Child in Foster Care: *A Story of Resilience* (Book)

A Gifted Child in Foster Care: *Student Workbook*

A Gifted Child in Foster Care: *Teacher's Guide*

Tapping into the Gifts, Talents, and Learning Styles of Special Education Students (Book)

Understanding Each Other: *A Guide for Parents and their Children* (Book)

Sexual Purity and the Young Woman: *A Guide to Sexual Purity*
(A reference book for teen and college-age girls)

An Urgent Call to the Power of Ministry: *Realizing your ministry through your life experiences*

More Than Mere Words: *Poetry That Ministers* (Christian Poetry Book)

Diversity and my Credit Union: *A True Story* (Book)

My Automobile Dealership: *A True Story* (Book)

Writer's Breakthrough: *Steps to Copyright and Publish Your Own Book*
(Book and CD)

How Can Jesus Be God? (Children's Book)

Poetic Book Series
Diversity in our Schools
Diversity in our Workplace
The Bad Butt Kids
He's Worth It
Our Employees…Our Cornerstones

Poetic Empowerment (Spoken Word CD)

Songs by Grace LaJoy (Music CD)

To learn more please visit us online at www.gracelajoy.com

Notes

Notes

Notes

Notes

Notes

Notes